BEYOND ChatGPT

Prompt Engineering Journal for Tweens 10-13

Build Real AI Skills With Tips, Challenges & Practice

MY PROJECT PROMPTS

NAME: ______________________________

DATE: ________________

THROUGH ______________

____

JOURNAL #_____ OF ______

MEMOS:______________________________

____

____

____

____

Let's Make Someone's Day - Together!

★ ★ ★ ★ ★

Hi family! I have a tiny favor that makes a BIG difference. Leaving a quick review for this journal helps other parents and tweens decide if it's the right fit for their tech-learning adventure. As you use this journal, please keep my request in mind.

Why bother?

- It shows kindness and helps beginners feel brave.
- It supports teaching how to create cool tools like this.
- It proves that sharing good vibes matters - yes, even online!

How long does it take?

Less than a minute. Seriously. And it can help someone else feel confident about learning AI.

Here's what your review can do:

- Help another family start their journey.
- Keep creative projects alive.
- Show your tween that small actions make a big impact.

Ready to spread some good karma?

Type this link in your browser, https://bit.ly/4pWHg4h

or Scan the QR code:

Scan me

P.S. Check out the other adults and teens journals also.
Something for the whole tech-savvy family!

HOW TO USE THIS JOURNAL

Welcome to your AI Helper Journal!

This journal teaches you how to talk to AI so it gives you exactly what you want. AI is like a super smart helper, but you need to tell it clearly what you need. The better you explain things, the better help you get!

Each time you use this journal, you fill out 2 pages:

Page 1: Plan What You Want - Think about what you need help with. Pick what kind of helper AI should be (like a teacher, friend, or story helper). Choose how it should sound (fun, encouraging, simple). Decide what your answer should look like (a list, steps, or paragraphs). Write down any special rules.

Page 2: Write Your Instructions - This is where you tell AI exactly what to do. Show examples of what you want and what you don't want. Write your steps. Then write your full instructions in the prompt box. After you try it, write down what worked and what you want to change next time.

This journal helps you:

- Get better answers from AI
- Learn cool new ways to ask for help
- Save your best ideas to use again
- See yourself getting better at this
- Have fun creating awesome projects

Check out the sample pages to see how other kids used this journal. Then start filling out your own pages!

SAMPLE 1: Science Fair Ideas
SAMPLE 2: Story About a Magic Backpack
SAMPLE 3: Learning Fractions
SAMPLE 4: Fun Video Ideas for YouTube

The more you practice, the better you'll get at telling AI what you need. Soon you'll be an expert at getting amazing help with all your projects!

Have fun and be creative!

SAMPLE 1: Science Fair Ideas

WHAT DO I WANT HELP WITH:
Get fun ideas for my science fair project about plants or animals
AI SHOULD ACT LIKE:
A Science Teacher who makes learning fun and exciting

PICK A HELPER:
☐ ✓ Friendly Teacher
☐ ✓ Creative Friend
☐ Story Helper
☐ Homework Buddy
☐ Other: _______________

HOW SHOULD IT SOUND:
☐ ✓ Fun and Friendly
☐ ✓ Excited and Encouraging
☐ Simple and Clear
☐ Super Creative
☐ Like a Real Expert

HOW SHOULD IT LOOK:
☐ ✓ List with dots
☐ List with numbers
☐ Short paragraphs
☐ Step by step
☐ Table or chart

WHO IS THIS FOR:
Me, a 6th grader who loves animals and wants to do something cool

SPECIAL RULES:
Keep it simple so I can actually do it
Make sure it is safe and does not cost too much money

MY NOTES:
Science fair is in 3 weeks. I need something I can set up and test at home. I want to learn something new and surprise my teacher!

SAMPLE 1: Science Fair Ideas

PROJECT NAME:
Awesome Science Fair Project Ideas
DATE: 02 01 2025 TRY NUMBER: 1

WHAT I WANT AI TO DO:
Give me 5 cool science fair project ideas about plants or animals that I can do at home in 3 weeks

MORE DETAILS:
I love animals and have a dog. I also like plants. The project needs to be something I can test or observe. It should be safe and not expensive.

SHOW AN EXAMPLE:
Good example: How music affects plant growth (I can test this at home)

Bad example: Building a rocket (too hard and dangerous)

MY STEPS:

1. Think about what I like (plants and animals)
2. Get 5 different ideas
3. Make sure each idea explains what to test
4. Pick the coolest one to actually do

MY PROMPT TO AI:
Act like a fun Science Teacher. Give me 5 science fair project ideas about plants or animals that I can do at home in 3 weeks. I am in 6th grade and love animals. Make each idea safe and not expensive. Explain what I would test or observe. Use a list with dots. Keep it exciting and friendly.

HOW IT WENT:
What was cool: Got ideas I never thought of! They were easy to understand.
What needs fixing: Some ideas needed materials I do not have
Next time I will: Ask AI to only use stuff I already have at home.

SAMPLE 2: Story About a Magic Backpack

WHAT DO I WANT HELP WITH:
Write a fun adventure story about a kid who finds a magic backpack

AI SHOULD ACT LIKE:
A Creative Story Writer who loves adventures and surprises

PICK A HELPER:

- ☐ ✓ Friendly Teacher
- ☐ ✓ Creative Friend
- ☐ ✓Story Helper
- ☐ ✓Homework Buddy
- ☐ ✓Other:___________

HOW SHOULD IT SOUND:

- ☐ ✓ Fun and Friendly
- ☐ Excited and Encouraging
- ☐ Simple and Clear
- ☐ ✓ Super Creative
- ☐ Like a Real Expert

HOW SHOULD IT LOOK:

- ☐ List with dots
- ☐ List with numbers
- ☐ ✓ Short paragraphs
- ☐ Step by step
- ☐ Table or chart

WHO IS THIS FOR:
Kids my age (10-13) who love adventure and magic stories

SPECIAL RULES:
Make it exciting but not scary
Keep the story around 300 words so I can read it in one sitting

MY NOTES:
I want a story I can share with my friends. The backpack should have cool powers and the main character should be brave and funny.

SAMPLE 2: Story About a Magic Backpack

PROJECT NAME:
The Magic Backpack Adventure
DATE: 02 05 2025   TRY NUMBER: 1

WHAT I WANT AI TO DO:
Write a short adventure story (about 300 words) about a kid who finds a magic backpack with special powers

MORE DETAILS:
The story should be exciting but not scary. The main character should be brave and funny. The backpack should have at least 2 cool powers.

SHOW AN EXAMPLE:
Good example: The backpack lets you fly and talk to animals

Bad example: The backpack is cursed and causes problems (too scary)

MY STEPS:
1. Start with how the kid finds the backpack
2. Show what powers the backpack has
3. Create an adventure where the kid uses the powers
4. End with a fun twist or happy ending

MY PROMPT TO AI:
Act like a Creative Story Writer who loves adventures. Write a 300 word story about a kid who finds a magic backpack. The backpack should have 2 cool powers. Make the main character brave and funny. Keep it exciting but not scary. Write in short paragraphs that are easy to read. Make it fun and creative.

HOW IT WENT:
What was cool: The story was super fun and my friends loved it!

What needs fixing: It was a little longer than 300 words

Next time I will: Ask for exactly 300 words or less

SAMPLE 3: Learning Fractions

WHAT DO I WANT HELP WITH:

Understand how to add fractions with different bottom numbers

AI SHOULD ACT LIKE:

A Patient Math Tutor who explains things in simple ways

PICK A ✓ HELPER

- ☐ ✓ Friendly Teacher
- ☐ ✓ Creative Friend
- ☐ ✓ Story Helper
- ☐ ✓ Homework Buddy
- ☐ ✓ Other:___________

HOW SHOULD IT SOUND:

- ☐ Fun and Friendly
- ☐ ✓ Excited and Encouraging
- ☐ ✓ Simple and Clear
- ☐ Super Creative
- ☐ Like a Real Expert

HOW SHOULD IT LOOK:

- ☐ List with dots
- ☐ List with numbers
- ☐ Short paragraphs
- ☐ ✓ Step by step
- ☐ Table or chart

WHO IS THIS FOR:

Me, a 5th grader who gets confused with fractions homework

SPECIAL RULES:

Use easy words and simple examples
Show me how to do it step by step with numbers I can practice

MY NOTES:

I understand adding fractions when the bottom numbers are the same. But when they are different, I get stuck. Need help before my test on Friday!

SAMPLE 3: Learning Fractions

PROJECT NAME:
Adding Fractions Made Easy
DATE: 02 10 2025   TRY NUMBER: 1

WHAT I WANT AI TO DO:
Teach me how to add fractions when the bottom numbers (denominators) are different, using simple steps and examples

MORE DETAILS:
I already know how to add fractions with the same bottom number. I need to learn the trick for when they are different. Use easy examples I can practice.

SHOW AN EXAMPLE:
Good example: 1/2 + 1/4 with clear steps showing how to solve it

Bad example: Really hard fractions like 7/13 + 5/17 (too confusing)

MY STEPS:
1. Explain what to do in simple words
2. Show me step by step with an easy example
3. Give me 2 more examples to try on my own
4. Make sure I understand before moving on

MY PROMPT TO AI:
Act like a Patient Math Tutor. Teach me how to add fractions with different bottom numbers. I am in 5th grade. Use simple words and easy examples like 1/2 + 1/4. Show me step by step how to solve it. Then give me 2 practice problems to try. Keep your explanation clear and encouraging.

HOW IT WENT:
What was cool: The steps were super clear and I finally get it!

What needs fixing: I want more practice problems

Next time I will: Ask for 5 practice problems with answers

SAMPLE 4: Fun Video Ideas for YouTube

WHAT DO I WANT HELP WITH:
Get ideas for fun videos I can make about arts and crafts or DIY projects

AI SHOULD ACT LIKE:
A Fun Video Creator Coach who loves arts and crafts

PICK A HELPER:
☐ Friendly Teacher
☐ ✓ Creative Friend
☐ Story Helper
☐ Homework Buddy
☐ ✓ Other: Video Coach

HOW SHOULD IT SOUND:
☐ ✓ Fun and Friendly
☐ ✓ Excited and Encouraging
☐ Simple and Clear
☐ ✓ Super Creative
☐ Like a Real Expert

HOW SHOULD IT LOOK:
☐ ✓ List with dots
☐ List with numbers
☐ ✓ Short paragraphs
☐ Step by step
☐ Table or chart

WHO IS THIS FOR:
Kids ages 10-13 who like making things and watching craft videos

SPECIAL RULES:
Keep ideas simple and use stuff I can find at home
Make the projects something I can finish in one afternoon

MY NOTES:
I want to start a YouTube channel with my best friend. We love making bracelets, decorating stuff, and cool art projects. Need ideas that look awesome on camera!

SAMPLE 4: Fun Video Ideas for YouTube

PROJECT NAME:
Awesome DIY Video Ideas
DATE: 02 14 2025   TRY NUMBER: 1

WHAT I WANT AI TO DO:
Give me 8 fun DIY and craft video ideas that I can film for a YouTube channel with my friend

MORE DETAILS:
My friend and I are starting a YouTube channel. We like making bracelets, decorating things, and doing art. Ideas should use materials we can find at home.

SHOW AN EXAMPLE:
Good example: How to make friendship bracelets in 10 minutes

Bad example: Building furniture (too hard and we do not have tools)

MY STEPS:

1. Think about what we like to make
2. Get 8 different video ideas
3. Make sure each idea is quick and looks cool on camera
4. Pick our favorites and start filming

MY PROMPT TO AI:
Act like a Fun Video Creator Coach who loves arts and crafts. Give me 8 DIY video ideas for a YouTube channel. My friend and I are ages 10-12 and we like making bracelets, decorating stuff, and doing art. Use materials we can find at home. Each project should take one afternoon or less. Keep it fun, creative, and exciting. Use a list with dots and short descriptions.

HOW IT WENT:
What was cool: We got so many ideas! Some are perfect for our first videos.

What needs fixing: A couple ideas needed special supplies we do not have

Next time I will: Ask for ideas using only paper, markers, and string

MY AI HELPER GUIDE

WHAT DO I WANT HELP WITH:

____

AI SHOULD ACT LIKE:

____

PICK A HELPER:

- ☐ Friendly Teacher
- ☐ Creative Friend
- ☐ Story Helper
- ☐ Homework Buddy
- ☐ Other: ______________

HOW SHOULD IT SOUND:

- ☐ Fun and Friendly
- ☐ Excited and Encouraging
- ☐ Simple and Clear
- ☐ Super Creative
- ☐ Like a Real Expert

HOW SHOULD IT LOOK:

- ☐ List with dots
- ☐ List with numbers
- ☐ Short paragraphs
- ☐ Step by step
- ☐ Table or chart

WHO IS THIS FOR:

____

SPECIAL RULES:

____

____

MY NOTES:

____

____

MY AI HELPER GUIDE

PROJECT NAME:

____

DATE: ____________ TRY NUMBER: ____________

WHAT I WANT AI TO DO:

____

____

MORE DETAILS:

____

____

SHOW AN EXAMPLE:

Good example: ________________________________

____

Bad Example: _________________________________

____

MY STEPS: ________________________________

____

____

MY PROMPT TO AI:

____

____

____

____

HOW IT WENT:

What was cool: _______________________________

What needs fixing: ____________________________

Next time I will: _____________________________

MY NOTES:

____

____

MY AI HELPER GUIDE

WHAT DO I WANT HELP WITH:

____

AI SHOULD ACT LIKE:

____

PICK A HELPER:

- ☐ Friendly Teacher
- ☐ Creative Friend
- ☐ Story Helper
- ☐ Homework Buddy
- ☐ Other: ______________

HOW SHOULD IT SOUND:

- ☐ Fun and Friendly
- ☐ Excited and Encouraging
- ☐ Simple and Clear
- ☐ Super Creative
- ☐ Like a Real Expert

HOW SHOULD IT LOOK:

- ☐ List with dots
- ☐ List with numbers
- ☐ Short paragraphs
- ☐ Step by step
- ☐ Table or chart

WHO IS THIS FOR:

____

SPECIAL RULES:

____

____

MY NOTES:

____

____

MY AI HELPER GUIDE

PROJECT NAME:

____

DATE: ____________ TRY NUMBER: ____________

WHAT I WANT AI TO DO:

____

____

MORE DETAILS:

____

____

SHOW AN EXAMPLE:

Good example: ______________________________

____

Bad Example: _______________________________

____

MY STEPS: ________________________________

____

____

MY PROMPT TO AI:

____

____

____

____

HOW IT WENT:

What was cool: ______________________________

What needs fixing: ___________________________

Next time I will: _____________________________

MY NOTES:

____

____

MY AI HELPER GUIDE

WHAT DO I WANT HELP WITH:

____

AI SHOULD ACT LIKE:

____

PICK A HELPER:

☐ Friendly Teacher
☐ Creative Friend
☐ Story Helper
☐ Homework Buddy
☐ Other: ________________

HOW SHOULD IT SOUND:

☐ Fun and Friendly
☐ Excited and Encouraging
☐ Simple and Clear
☐ Super Creative
☐ Like a Real Expert

HOW SHOULD IT LOOK:

☐ List with dots
☐ List with numbers
☐ Short paragraphs
☐ Step by step
☐ Table or chart

WHO IS THIS FOR:

____

SPECIAL RULES:

____

____

MY NOTES:

____

____

MY AI HELPER GUIDE

PROJECT NAME:

____

DATE: ______________ TRY NUMBER: ______________

WHAT I WANT AI TO DO:

____

____

MORE DETAILS:

____

____

SHOW AN EXAMPLE:

Good example: ______________________________________

____

Bad Example: ______________________________________

____

MY STEPS: ______________________________________

____

____

MY PROMPT TO AI:

____

____

____

____

HOW IT WENT:

What was cool: ______________________________________

What needs fixing: ______________________________________

Next time I will: ______________________________________

MY NOTES:

____

____

MY AI HELPER GUIDE

WHAT DO I WANT HELP WITH:

____

AI SHOULD ACT LIKE:

____

PICK A HELPER:

☐ Friendly Teacher
☐ Creative Friend
☐ Story Helper
☐ Homework Buddy
☐ Other: ____________

HOW SHOULD IT SOUND:

☐ Fun and Friendly
☐ Excited and Encouraging
☐ Simple and Clear
☐ Super Creative
☐ Like a Real Expert

HOW SHOULD IT LOOK:

☐ List with dots
☐ List with numbers
☐ Short paragraphs
☐ Step by step
☐ Table or chart

WHO IS THIS FOR:

____

SPECIAL RULES:

____

____

MY NOTES:

____

____

MY AI HELPER GUIDE

PROJECT NAME: ______________________________

DATE: ____________ TRY NUMBER: ____________

WHAT I WANT AI TO DO:

____

____

MORE DETAILS:

____

____

SHOW AN EXAMPLE:

Good example: ______________________________

____

Bad Example: ______________________________

____

MY STEPS: ______________________________

____

____

MY PROMPT TO AI:

____

____

____

____

HOW IT WENT:

What was cool: ______________________________

What needs fixing: ______________________________

Next time I will: ______________________________

MY NOTES:

____

____

MY AI HELPER GUIDE

WHAT DO I WANT HELP WITH:

____

AI SHOULD ACT LIKE:

____

PICK A HELPER:

☐ Friendly Teacher
☐ Creative Friend
☐ Story Helper
☐ Homework Buddy
☐ Other: ______________

HOW SHOULD IT SOUND:

☐ Fun and Friendly
☐ Excited and Encouraging
☐ Simple and Clear
☐ Super Creative
☐ Like a Real Expert

HOW SHOULD IT LOOK:

☐ List with dots
☐ List with numbers
☐ Short paragraphs
☐ Step by step
☐ Table or chart

WHO IS THIS FOR:

____

SPECIAL RULES:

____

____

MY NOTES:

____

____

MY AI HELPER GUIDE

PROJECT NAME:

____

DATE: ____________ TRY NUMBER: ____________

WHAT I WANT AI TO DO:

____

____

MORE DETAILS:

____

____

SHOW AN EXAMPLE:

Good example: ______________________________

____

Bad Example: _______________________________

____

MY STEPS: ________________________________

____

____

MY PROMPT TO AI:

____

____

____

____

HOW IT WENT:

What was cool: ______________________________

What needs fixing: ___________________________

Next time I will: _____________________________

MY NOTES:

____

____

MY AI HELPER GUIDE

WHAT DO I WANT HELP WITH:

____

AI SHOULD ACT LIKE:

____

PICK A HELPER:

☐ Friendly Teacher
☐ Creative Friend
☐ Story Helper
☐ Homework Buddy
☐ Other: ____________

HOW SHOULD IT SOUND:

☐ Fun and Friendly
☐ Excited and Encouraging
☐ Simple and Clear
☐ Super Creative
☐ Like a Real Expert

HOW SHOULD IT LOOK:

☐ List with dots
☐ List with numbers
☐ Short paragraphs
☐ Step by step
☐ Table or chart

WHO IS THIS FOR:

____

SPECIAL RULES:

____

____

MY NOTES:

____

____

MY AI HELPER GUIDE

PROJECT NAME:

____

DATE: ____________ TRY NUMBER: ____________

WHAT I WANT AI TO DO:

____

____

MORE DETAILS:

____

____

SHOW AN EXAMPLE:

Good example: ______________________________________

____

Bad Example: ______________________________________

____

MY STEPS: ______________________________________

____

____

MY PROMPT TO AI:

____

____

____

____

HOW IT WENT:

What was cool:______________________________________

What needs fixing: __________________________________

Next time I will:____________________________________

MY NOTES:

____

____

MY AI HELPER GUIDE

WHAT DO I WANT HELP WITH:

____

AI SHOULD ACT LIKE:

____

PICK A HELPER:

- ☐ Friendly Teacher
- ☐ Creative Friend
- ☐ Story Helper
- ☐ Homework Buddy
- ☐ Other: ______________

HOW SHOULD IT SOUND:

- ☐ Fun and Friendly
- ☐ Excited and Encouraging
- ☐ Simple and Clear
- ☐ Super Creative
- ☐ Like a Real Expert

HOW SHOULD IT LOOK:

- ☐ List with dots
- ☐ List with numbers
- ☐ Short paragraphs
- ☐ Step by step
- ☐ Table or chart

WHO IS THIS FOR:

____

SPECIAL RULES:

____

____

MY NOTES:

____

____

MY AI HELPER GUIDE

PROJECT NAME:

____

DATE: ____________ TRY NUMBER: ____________

WHAT I WANT AI TO DO:

____

____

MORE DETAILS:

____

____

SHOW AN EXAMPLE:

Good example: ________________________________

____

Bad Example: _________________________________

____

MY STEPS: ________________________________

____

____

MY PROMPT TO AI:

____

____

____

____

HOW IT WENT:

What was cool:________________________________

What needs fixing: ____________________________

Next time I will:______________________________

MY NOTES:

____

____

MY AI HELPER GUIDE

WHAT DO I WANT HELP WITH:

____

AI SHOULD ACT LIKE:

____

PICK A HELPER:

- ☐ Friendly Teacher
- ☐ Creative Friend
- ☐ Story Helper
- ☐ Homework Buddy
- ☐ Other: ______________

HOW SHOULD IT SOUND:

- ☐ Fun and Friendly
- ☐ Excited and Encouraging
- ☐ Simple and Clear
- ☐ Super Creative
- ☐ Like a Real Expert

HOW SHOULD IT LOOK:

- ☐ List with dots
- ☐ List with numbers
- ☐ Short paragraphs
- ☐ Step by step
- ☐ Table or chart

WHO IS THIS FOR:

____

SPECIAL RULES:

____

____

MY NOTES:

____

____

MY AI HELPER GUIDE

PROJECT NAME:

____

DATE: ____________ TRY NUMBER: ____________

WHAT I WANT AI TO DO:

____

____

MORE DETAILS:

____

____

SHOW AN EXAMPLE:

Good example: ________________________________

____

Bad Example: _________________________________

____

MY STEPS: ________________________________

____

____

MY PROMPT TO AI:

____

____

____

____

HOW IT WENT:

What was cool: _______________________________

What needs fixing: ___________________________

Next time I will: ____________________________

MY NOTES:

____

____

MY AI HELPER GUIDE

WHAT DO I WANT HELP WITH:

____

AI SHOULD ACT LIKE:

____

PICK A HELPER:

- ☐ Friendly Teacher
- ☐ Creative Friend
- ☐ Story Helper
- ☐ Homework Buddy
- ☐ Other: ________________

HOW SHOULD IT SOUND:

- ☐ Fun and Friendly
- ☐ Excited and Encouraging
- ☐ Simple and Clear
- ☐ Super Creative
- ☐ Like a Real Expert

HOW SHOULD IT LOOK:

- ☐ List with dots
- ☐ List with numbers
- ☐ Short paragraphs
- ☐ Step by step
- ☐ Table or chart

WHO IS THIS FOR:

____

SPECIAL RULES:

____

____

MY NOTES:

____

____

MY AI HELPER GUIDE

PROJECT NAME:

____

DATE: ______________ TRY NUMBER: ______________

WHAT I WANT AI TO DO:

____

____

MORE DETAILS:

____

____

SHOW AN EXAMPLE:

Good example: ______________________________________

____

Bad Example: ______________________________________

____

MY STEPS: ______________________________________

____

____

MY PROMPT TO AI:

____

____

____

____

HOW IT WENT:

What was cool: ______________________________________

What needs fixing: ______________________________________

Next time I will: ______________________________________

MY NOTES:

____

____

MY AI HELPER GUIDE

WHAT DO I WANT HELP WITH:

____

AI SHOULD ACT LIKE:

____

PICK A HELPER:

☐ Friendly Teacher
☐ Creative Friend
☐ Story Helper
☐ Homework Buddy
☐ Other: ____________

HOW SHOULD IT SOUND:

☐ Fun and Friendly
☐ Excited and Encouraging
☐ Simple and Clear
☐ Super Creative
☐ Like a Real Expert

HOW SHOULD IT LOOK:

☐ List with dots
☐ List with numbers
☐ Short paragraphs
☐ Step by step
☐ Table or chart

WHO IS THIS FOR:

____

SPECIAL RULES:

____

____

MY NOTES:

____

____

MY AI HELPER GUIDE

PROJECT NAME:

____

DATE: ______________ TRY NUMBER: ______________

WHAT I WANT AI TO DO:

____

____

MORE DETAILS:

____

____

SHOW AN EXAMPLE:

Good example: ___________________________________

____

Bad Example: ___________________________________

____

MY STEPS: ___________________________________

____

____

MY PROMPT TO AI:

____

____

____

____

HOW IT WENT:

What was cool: __________________________________

What needs fixing: _______________________________

Next time I will: _________________________________

MY NOTES:

____

____

MY AI HELPER GUIDE

WHAT DO I WANT HELP WITH:

____

AI SHOULD ACT LIKE:

____

PICK A HELPER:

- ☐ Friendly Teacher
- ☐ Creative Friend
- ☐ Story Helper
- ☐ Homework Buddy
- ☐ Other: _______________

HOW SHOULD IT SOUND:

- ☐ Fun and Friendly
- ☐ Excited and Encouraging
- ☐ Simple and Clear
- ☐ Super Creative
- ☐ Like a Real Expert

HOW SHOULD IT LOOK:

- ☐ List with dots
- ☐ List with numbers
- ☐ Short paragraphs
- ☐ Step by step
- ☐ Table or chart

WHO IS THIS FOR:

____

SPECIAL RULES:

____

____

MY NOTES:

____

____

MY AI HELPER GUIDE

PROJECT NAME:

____

DATE: ______________ TRY NUMBER: ______________

WHAT I WANT AI TO DO:

____

____

MORE DETAILS:

____

____

SHOW AN EXAMPLE:

Good example: ____

____

Bad Example: ____

____

MY STEPS: ____

____

____

MY PROMPT TO AI:

____

____

____

____

HOW IT WENT:

What was cool: ____

What needs fixing: ____

Next time I will: ____

MY NOTES:

____

____

MY AI HELPER GUIDE

WHAT DO I WANT HELP WITH:

____

AI SHOULD ACT LIKE:

____

PICK A HELPER:

☐ Friendly Teacher
☐ Creative Friend
☐ Story Helper
☐ Homework Buddy
☐ Other: ____________

HOW SHOULD IT SOUND:

☐ Fun and Friendly
☐ Excited and Encouraging
☐ Simple and Clear
☐ Super Creative
☐ Like a Real Expert

HOW SHOULD IT LOOK:

☐ List with dots
☐ List with numbers
☐ Short paragraphs
☐ Step by step
☐ Table or chart

WHO IS THIS FOR:

____

SPECIAL RULES:

____

____

MY NOTES:

____

____

MY AI HELPER GUIDE

PROJECT NAME:

____

DATE: ______________ TRY NUMBER: ______________

WHAT I WANT AI TO DO:

____

____

MORE DETAILS:

____

____

SHOW AN EXAMPLE:

Good example: ____

____

Bad Example: ____

____

MY STEPS: ____

____

____

MY PROMPT TO AI:

____

____

____

____

HOW IT WENT:

What was cool: ____

What needs fixing: ____

Next time I will: ____

MY NOTES:

____

____

MY AI HELPER GUIDE

WHAT DO I WANT HELP WITH:

____

AI SHOULD ACT LIKE:

____

PICK A HELPER:

- ☐ Friendly Teacher
- ☐ Creative Friend
- ☐ Story Helper
- ☐ Homework Buddy
- ☐ Other: ______________

HOW SHOULD IT SOUND:

- ☐ Fun and Friendly
- ☐ Excited and Encouraging
- ☐ Simple and Clear
- ☐ Super Creative
- ☐ Like a Real Expert

HOW SHOULD IT LOOK:

- ☐ List with dots
- ☐ List with numbers
- ☐ Short paragraphs
- ☐ Step by step
- ☐ Table or chart

WHO IS THIS FOR:

____

SPECIAL RULES:

____

____

MY NOTES:

____

____

MY AI HELPER GUIDE

PROJECT NAME:

____

DATE: ______________ TRY NUMBER: ______________

WHAT I WANT AI TO DO:

____

____

MORE DETAILS:

____

____

SHOW AN EXAMPLE:

Good example: ______________________________________

____

Bad Example: ______________________________________

____

MY STEPS: ______________________________________

____

____

MY PROMPT TO AI:

____

____

____

____

HOW IT WENT:

What was cool: ______________________________________

What needs fixing: ______________________________________

Next time I will: ______________________________________

MY NOTES:

____

____

MY AI HELPER GUIDE

WHAT DO I WANT HELP WITH:

____

AI SHOULD ACT LIKE:

____

PICK A HELPER:

- ☐ Friendly Teacher
- ☐ Creative Friend
- ☐ Story Helper
- ☐ Homework Buddy
- ☐ Other: ______________

HOW SHOULD IT SOUND:

- ☐ Fun and Friendly
- ☐ Excited and Encouraging
- ☐ Simple and Clear
- ☐ Super Creative
- ☐ Like a Real Expert

HOW SHOULD IT LOOK:

- ☐ List with dots
- ☐ List with numbers
- ☐ Short paragraphs
- ☐ Step by step
- ☐ Table or chart

WHO IS THIS FOR:

____

SPECIAL RULES:

____

____

MY NOTES:

____

____

MY AI HELPER GUIDE

PROJECT NAME:

____

DATE: _____________ TRY NUMBER: _____________

WHAT I WANT AI TO DO:

____

____

MORE DETAILS:

____

____

SHOW AN EXAMPLE:

Good example: ____

____

Bad Example: ____

____

MY STEPS: ____

____

____

MY PROMPT TO AI:

____

____

____

____

HOW IT WENT:

What was cool:____

What needs fixing: ____

Next time I will:____

MY NOTES:

____

____

MY AI HELPER GUIDE

WHAT DO I WANT HELP WITH:

____

AI SHOULD ACT LIKE:

____

PICK A HELPER:

☐ Friendly Teacher
☐ Creative Friend
☐ Story Helper
☐ Homework Buddy
☐ Other: ________________

HOW SHOULD IT SOUND:

☐ Fun and Friendly
☐ Excited and Encouraging
☐ Simple and Clear
☐ Super Creative
☐ Like a Real Expert

HOW SHOULD IT LOOK:

☐ List with dots
☐ List with numbers
☐ Short paragraphs
☐ Step by step
☐ Table or chart

WHO IS THIS FOR:

____

SPECIAL RULES:

____
____

MY NOTES:

____
____

MY AI HELPER GUIDE

PROJECT NAME:

____

DATE: ____________ TRY NUMBER: ____________

WHAT I WANT AI TO DO:

____

____

MORE DETAILS:

____

____

SHOW AN EXAMPLE:

Good example: ______________________________

____

Bad Example: ______________________________

____

MY STEPS: ______________________________

____

____

MY PROMPT TO AI:

____

____

____

____

HOW IT WENT:

What was cool: ______________________________

What needs fixing: ______________________________

Next time I will: ______________________________

MY NOTES:

____

____

MY AI HELPER GUIDE

WHAT DO I WANT HELP WITH:

____

AI SHOULD ACT LIKE:

____

PICK A HELPER:

☐ Friendly Teacher
☐ Creative Friend
☐ Story Helper
☐ Homework Buddy
☐ Other: ________________

HOW SHOULD IT SOUND:

☐ Fun and Friendly
☐ Excited and Encouraging
☐ Simple and Clear
☐ Super Creative
☐ Like a Real Expert

HOW SHOULD IT LOOK:

☐ List with dots
☐ List with numbers
☐ Short paragraphs
☐ Step by step
☐ Table or chart

WHO IS THIS FOR:

____

SPECIAL RULES:

____

____

MY NOTES:

____

____

MY AI HELPER GUIDE

PROJECT NAME:

____

DATE: ______________ TRY NUMBER: ______________

WHAT I WANT AI TO DO:

____

____

MORE DETAILS:

____

____

SHOW AN EXAMPLE:

Good example: ______________________________

____

Bad Example: _______________________________

____

MY STEPS: _________________________________

____

____

MY PROMPT TO AI:

____

____

____

____

HOW IT WENT:

What was cool: ______________________________

What needs fixing: ___________________________

Next time I will: ____________________________

MY NOTES:

____

____

MY AI HELPER GUIDE

WHAT DO I WANT HELP WITH:

____

AI SHOULD ACT LIKE:

____

PICK A HELPER:

☐ Friendly Teacher
☐ Creative Friend
☐ Story Helper
☐ Homework Buddy
☐ Other: ______________

HOW SHOULD IT SOUND:

☐ Fun and Friendly
☐ Excited and Encouraging
☐ Simple and Clear
☐ Super Creative
☐ Like a Real Expert

HOW SHOULD IT LOOK:

☐ List with dots
☐ List with numbers
☐ Short paragraphs
☐ Step by step
☐ Table or chart

WHO IS THIS FOR:

____

SPECIAL RULES:

____

____

MY NOTES:

____

____

MY AI HELPER GUIDE

PROJECT NAME:

____

DATE: ______________ TRY NUMBER: ______________

WHAT I WANT AI TO DO:

____

____

MORE DETAILS:

____

____

SHOW AN EXAMPLE:

Good example: ______________________________________

____

Bad Example: ______________________________________

____

MY STEPS: ______________________________________

____

____

MY PROMPT TO AI:

____

____

____

____

HOW IT WENT:

What was cool: ______________________________________

What needs fixing: ______________________________________

Next time I will: ______________________________________

MY NOTES:

____

____

MY AI HELPER GUIDE

WHAT DO I WANT HELP WITH:

____

AI SHOULD ACT LIKE:

____

PICK A HELPER:

☐ Friendly Teacher
☐ Creative Friend
☐ Story Helper
☐ Homework Buddy
☐ Other: ______________

HOW SHOULD IT SOUND:

☐ Fun and Friendly
☐ Excited and Encouraging
☐ Simple and Clear
☐ Super Creative
☐ Like a Real Expert

HOW SHOULD IT LOOK:

☐ List with dots
☐ List with numbers
☐ Short paragraphs
☐ Step by step
☐ Table or chart

WHO IS THIS FOR:

____

SPECIAL RULES:

____

____

MY NOTES:

____

____

MY AI HELPER GUIDE

PROJECT NAME:

____

DATE: ____________ TRY NUMBER: ____________

WHAT I WANT AI TO DO:

____

____

MORE DETAILS:

____

____

SHOW AN EXAMPLE:

Good example: ________________________________

____

Bad Example: ________________________________

____

MY STEPS: ________________________________

____

____

MY PROMPT TO AI:

____

____

____

____

HOW IT WENT:

What was cool: _______________________________

What needs fixing: ____________________________

Next time I will: _____________________________

MY NOTES:

____

____

MY AI HELPER GUIDE

WHAT DO I WANT HELP WITH:

____

AI SHOULD ACT LIKE:

____

PICK A HELPER:

- ☐ Friendly Teacher
- ☐ Creative Friend
- ☐ Story Helper
- ☐ Homework Buddy
- ☐ Other: ______________

HOW SHOULD IT SOUND:

- ☐ Fun and Friendly
- ☐ Excited and Encouraging
- ☐ Simple and Clear
- ☐ Super Creative
- ☐ Like a Real Expert

HOW SHOULD IT LOOK:

- ☐ List with dots
- ☐ List with numbers
- ☐ Short paragraphs
- ☐ Step by step
- ☐ Table or chart

WHO IS THIS FOR:

____

SPECIAL RULES:

____

____

MY NOTES:

____

MY AI HELPER GUIDE

PROJECT NAME: ____________________

DATE: ____________ TRY NUMBER: ____________

WHAT I WANT AI TO DO:

____

____

MORE DETAILS:

____

____

SHOW AN EXAMPLE:

Good example: ____________________

____

Bad Example: ____________________

____

MY STEPS: ____________________

____

____

MY PROMPT TO AI:

____

____

____

____

HOW IT WENT:

What was cool: ____________________

What needs fixing: ____________________

Next time I will: ____________________

MY NOTES:

____

____

MY AI HELPER GUIDE

WHAT DO I WANT HELP WITH:

____

AI SHOULD ACT LIKE:

____

PICK A HELPER:

- ☐ Friendly Teacher
- ☐ Creative Friend
- ☐ Story Helper
- ☐ Homework Buddy
- ☐ Other: ________________

HOW SHOULD IT SOUND:

- ☐ Fun and Friendly
- ☐ Excited and Encouraging
- ☐ Simple and Clear
- ☐ Super Creative
- ☐ Like a Real Expert

HOW SHOULD IT LOOK:

- ☐ List with dots
- ☐ List with numbers
- ☐ Short paragraphs
- ☐ Step by step
- ☐ Table or chart

WHO IS THIS FOR:

____

SPECIAL RULES:

____

____

MY NOTES:

____

____

MY AI HELPER GUIDE

PROJECT NAME:

____

DATE: ____________ TRY NUMBER: ____________

WHAT I WANT AI TO DO:

____

____

MORE DETAILS:

____

____

SHOW AN EXAMPLE:

Good example: ______________________________

____

Bad Example: ______________________________

____

MY STEPS: ______________________________

____

____

MY PROMPT TO AI:

____

____

____

____

HOW IT WENT:

What was cool: ______________________________

What needs fixing: ______________________________

Next time I will: ______________________________

MY NOTES:

____

____

MY AI HELPER GUIDE

WHAT DO I WANT HELP WITH:

____

AI SHOULD ACT LIKE:

____

PICK A HELPER:

☐ Friendly Teacher
☐ Creative Friend
☐ Story Helper
☐ Homework Buddy
☐ Other: ____________

HOW SHOULD IT SOUND:

☐ Fun and Friendly
☐ Excited and Encouraging
☐ Simple and Clear
☐ Super Creative
☐ Like a Real Expert

HOW SHOULD IT LOOK:

☐ List with dots
☐ List with numbers
☐ Short paragraphs
☐ Step by step
☐ Table or chart

WHO IS THIS FOR:

____

SPECIAL RULES:

____
____

MY NOTES:

____
____

MY AI HELPER GUIDE

PROJECT NAME:

____

DATE: ______________ TRY NUMBER: ______________

WHAT I WANT AI TO DO:

____

____

MORE DETAILS:

____

____

SHOW AN EXAMPLE:

Good example: ______________________________________

____

Bad Example: ______________________________________

____

MY STEPS: ______________________________________

____

____

MY PROMPT TO AI:

____

____

____

____

HOW IT WENT:

What was cool: ______________________________________

What needs fixing: ______________________________________

Next time I will: ______________________________________

MY NOTES:

____

____

MY AI HELPER GUIDE

WHAT DO I WANT HELP WITH:

____

AI SHOULD ACT LIKE:

____

PICK A HELPER:

- ☐ Friendly Teacher
- ☐ Creative Friend
- ☐ Story Helper
- ☐ Homework Buddy
- ☐ Other: ______________

HOW SHOULD IT SOUND:

- ☐ Fun and Friendly
- ☐ Excited and Encouraging
- ☐ Simple and Clear
- ☐ Super Creative
- ☐ Like a Real Expert

HOW SHOULD IT LOOK:

- ☐ List with dots
- ☐ List with numbers
- ☐ Short paragraphs
- ☐ Step by step
- ☐ Table or chart

WHO IS THIS FOR:

____

SPECIAL RULES:

____

____

MY NOTES:

____

____

MY AI HELPER GUIDE

PROJECT NAME:

____

DATE: ____________ TRY NUMBER: ____________

WHAT I WANT AI TO DO:

____

____

MORE DETAILS:

____

____

SHOW AN EXAMPLE:

Good example: ________________________________

____

Bad Example: _________________________________

____

MY STEPS: _________________________________

____

____

MY PROMPT TO AI:

____

____

____

____

HOW IT WENT:

What was cool: ________________________________

What needs fixing: _____________________________

Next time I will: ______________________________

MY NOTES:

____

____

MY AI HELPER GUIDE

WHAT DO I WANT HELP WITH:

____

AI SHOULD ACT LIKE:

____

PICK A HELPER:

- ☐ Friendly Teacher
- ☐ Creative Friend
- ☐ Story Helper
- ☐ Homework Buddy
- ☐ Other: ______________

HOW SHOULD IT SOUND:

- ☐ Fun and Friendly
- ☐ Excited and Encouraging
- ☐ Simple and Clear
- ☐ Super Creative
- ☐ Like a Real Expert

HOW SHOULD IT LOOK:

- ☐ List with dots
- ☐ List with numbers
- ☐ Short paragraphs
- ☐ Step by step
- ☐ Table or chart

WHO IS THIS FOR:

____

SPECIAL RULES:

____

____

MY NOTES:

____

____

MY AI HELPER GUIDE

PROJECT NAME:

____

DATE: ______________ TRY NUMBER: ______________

WHAT I WANT AI TO DO:

____

____

MORE DETAILS:

____

____

SHOW AN EXAMPLE:

Good example: ______________________________

____

Bad Example: _______________________________

____

MY STEPS: _______________________________

____

____

MY PROMPT TO AI:

____

____

____

____

HOW IT WENT:

What was cool:______________________________

What needs fixing: __________________________

Next time I will:____________________________

MY NOTES:

____

____

MY AI HELPER GUIDE

WHAT DO I WANT HELP WITH:

____

AI SHOULD ACT LIKE:

____

PICK A HELPER:

- ☐ Friendly Teacher
- ☐ Creative Friend
- ☐ Story Helper
- ☐ Homework Buddy
- ☐ Other: ________________

HOW SHOULD IT SOUND:

- ☐ Fun and Friendly
- ☐ Excited and Encouraging
- ☐ Simple and Clear
- ☐ Super Creative
- ☐ Like a Real Expert

HOW SHOULD IT LOOK:

- ☐ List with dots
- ☐ List with numbers
- ☐ Short paragraphs
- ☐ Step by step
- ☐ Table or chart

WHO IS THIS FOR:

____

SPECIAL RULES:

____

____

MY NOTES:

____

____

MY AI HELPER GUIDE

PROJECT NAME:

____

DATE: ____________ TRY NUMBER: ____________

WHAT I WANT AI TO DO:

____

____

MORE DETAILS:

____

____

SHOW AN EXAMPLE:

Good example: ________________________________

____

Bad Example: _________________________________

____

MY STEPS: ________________________________

____

____

MY PROMPT TO AI:

____

____

____

____

HOW IT WENT:

What was cool: _______________________________

What needs fixing: ___________________________

Next time I will: ____________________________

MY NOTES:

____

____

MY AI HELPER GUIDE

WHAT DO I WANT HELP WITH:

____

AI SHOULD ACT LIKE:

____

PICK A HELPER:

☐ Friendly Teacher
☐ Creative Friend
☐ Story Helper
☐ Homework Buddy
☐ Other: ______________

HOW SHOULD IT SOUND:

☐ Fun and Friendly
☐ Excited and Encouraging
☐ Simple and Clear
☐ Super Creative
☐ Like a Real Expert

HOW SHOULD IT LOOK:

☐ List with dots
☐ List with numbers
☐ Short paragraphs
☐ Step by step
☐ Table or chart

WHO IS THIS FOR:

____

SPECIAL RULES:

____

____

MY NOTES:

____

____

MY AI HELPER GUIDE

PROJECT NAME:

____

DATE: ______________ TRY NUMBER: ______________

WHAT I WANT AI TO DO:

____

____

MORE DETAILS:

____

____

SHOW AN EXAMPLE:

Good example: ______________________________

____

Bad Example: ______________________________

____

MY STEPS: ______________________________

____

____

MY PROMPT TO AI:

____

____

____

____

HOW IT WENT:

What was cool: ______________________________

What needs fixing: ______________________________

Next time I will: ______________________________

MY NOTES:

____

____

MY AI HELPER GUIDE

WHAT DO I WANT HELP WITH:

____

AI SHOULD ACT LIKE:

____

PICK A HELPER:

- ☐ Friendly Teacher
- ☐ Creative Friend
- ☐ Story Helper
- ☐ Homework Buddy
- ☐ Other: ______________

HOW SHOULD IT SOUND:

- ☐ Fun and Friendly
- ☐ Excited and Encouraging
- ☐ Simple and Clear
- ☐ Super Creative
- ☐ Like a Real Expert

HOW SHOULD IT LOOK:

- ☐ List with dots
- ☐ List with numbers
- ☐ Short paragraphs
- ☐ Step by step
- ☐ Table or chart

WHO IS THIS FOR:

____

SPECIAL RULES:

____

____

MY NOTES:

____

____

MY AI HELPER GUIDE

PROJECT NAME:

____

DATE: ____________ TRY NUMBER: ____________

WHAT I WANT AI TO DO:

____

____

MORE DETAILS:

____

____

SHOW AN EXAMPLE:

Good example: ______________________________

____

Bad Example: _______________________________

____

MY STEPS: ______________________________

____

____

MY PROMPT TO AI:

____

____

____

____

HOW IT WENT:

What was cool: _____________________________

What needs fixing: __________________________

Next time I will: ___________________________

MY NOTES:

____

____

MY AI HELPER GUIDE

WHAT DO I WANT HELP WITH:

____

AI SHOULD ACT LIKE:

____

PICK A HELPER:

- ☐ Friendly Teacher
- ☐ Creative Friend
- ☐ Story Helper
- ☐ Homework Buddy
- ☐ Other: ______________

HOW SHOULD IT SOUND:

- ☐ Fun and Friendly
- ☐ Excited and Encouraging
- ☐ Simple and Clear
- ☐ Super Creative
- ☐ Like a Real Expert

HOW SHOULD IT LOOK:

- ☐ List with dots
- ☐ List with numbers
- ☐ Short paragraphs
- ☐ Step by step
- ☐ Table or chart

WHO IS THIS FOR:

____

SPECIAL RULES:

____

____

MY NOTES:

____

____

MY AI HELPER GUIDE

PROJECT NAME:

____

DATE: ____________ TRY NUMBER: ____________

WHAT I WANT AI TO DO:

____

____

MORE DETAILS:

____

____

SHOW AN EXAMPLE:

Good example: ________________________________

____

Bad Example: _________________________________

____

MY STEPS: ________________________________

____

____

MY PROMPT TO AI:

____

____

____

____

HOW IT WENT:

What was cool: _______________________________

What needs fixing: ___________________________

Next time I will: _____________________________

MY NOTES:

____

____

MY AI HELPER GUIDE

WHAT DO I WANT HELP WITH:

____

AI SHOULD ACT LIKE:

____

PICK A HELPER:

- ☐ Friendly Teacher
- ☐ Creative Friend
- ☐ Story Helper
- ☐ Homework Buddy
- ☐ Other: ______________

HOW SHOULD IT SOUND:

- ☐ Fun and Friendly
- ☐ Excited and Encouraging
- ☐ Simple and Clear
- ☐ Super Creative
- ☐ Like a Real Expert

HOW SHOULD IT LOOK:

- ☐ List with dots
- ☐ List with numbers
- ☐ Short paragraphs
- ☐ Step by step
- ☐ Table or chart

WHO IS THIS FOR:

____

SPECIAL RULES:

____

____

MY NOTES:

____

____

MY AI HELPER GUIDE

PROJECT NAME:

____

DATE: ______________ TRY NUMBER: ______________

WHAT I WANT AI TO DO:

____

____

MORE DETAILS:

____

____

SHOW AN EXAMPLE:

Good example: ____

____

Bad Example: ____

____

MY STEPS: ____

____

____

MY PROMPT TO AI:

____

____

____

____

HOW IT WENT:

What was cool: ____

What needs fixing: ____

Next time I will: ____

MY NOTES:

____

____

MY AI HELPER GUIDE

WHAT DO I WANT HELP WITH:

____

AI SHOULD ACT LIKE:

____

PICK A HELPER:

- ☐ Friendly Teacher
- ☐ Creative Friend
- ☐ Story Helper
- ☐ Homework Buddy
- ☐ Other: ______________

HOW SHOULD IT SOUND:

- ☐ Fun and Friendly
- ☐ Excited and Encouraging
- ☐ Simple and Clear
- ☐ Super Creative
- ☐ Like a Real Expert

HOW SHOULD IT LOOK:

- ☐ List with dots
- ☐ List with numbers
- ☐ Short paragraphs
- ☐ Step by step
- ☐ Table or chart

WHO IS THIS FOR:

____

SPECIAL RULES:

____

____

MY NOTES:

____

____

MY AI HELPER GUIDE

PROJECT NAME:

____

DATE: ______________ TRY NUMBER: ______________

WHAT I WANT AI TO DO:

____

____

MORE DETAILS:

____

____

SHOW AN EXAMPLE:

Good example: ____

____

Bad Example: ____

____

MY STEPS: ____

____

____

MY PROMPT TO AI:

____

____

____

____

HOW IT WENT:

What was cool: ____

What needs fixing: ____

Next time I will: ____

MY NOTES:

____

____

MY AI HELPER GUIDE

WHAT DO I WANT HELP WITH:

____

AI SHOULD ACT LIKE:

____

PICK A HELPER:

- ☐ Friendly Teacher
- ☐ Creative Friend
- ☐ Story Helper
- ☐ Homework Buddy
- ☐ Other: ______________

HOW SHOULD IT SOUND:

- ☐ Fun and Friendly
- ☐ Excited and Encouraging
- ☐ Simple and Clear
- ☐ Super Creative
- ☐ Like a Real Expert

HOW SHOULD IT LOOK:

- ☐ List with dots
- ☐ List with numbers
- ☐ Short paragraphs
- ☐ Step by step
- ☐ Table or chart

WHO IS THIS FOR:

____

SPECIAL RULES:

____

____

MY NOTES:

____

____

MY AI HELPER GUIDE

PROJECT NAME:

____

DATE: ____________ TRY NUMBER: ____________

WHAT I WANT AI TO DO:

____

____

MORE DETAILS:

____

____

SHOW AN EXAMPLE:

Good example: ______________________________

____

Bad Example: ______________________________

____

MY STEPS: ______________________________

____

____

MY PROMPT TO AI:

____

____

____

____

HOW IT WENT:

What was cool: ______________________________

What needs fixing: ______________________________

Next time I will: ______________________________

MY NOTES:

____

____

MY AI HELPER GUIDE

WHAT DO I WANT HELP WITH:

____

AI SHOULD ACT LIKE:

____

PICK A HELPER:

- ☐ Friendly Teacher
- ☐ Creative Friend
- ☐ Story Helper
- ☐ Homework Buddy
- ☐ Other: ______________

HOW SHOULD IT SOUND:

- ☐ Fun and Friendly
- ☐ Excited and Encouraging
- ☐ Simple and Clear
- ☐ Super Creative
- ☐ Like a Real Expert

HOW SHOULD IT LOOK:

- ☐ List with dots
- ☐ List with numbers
- ☐ Short paragraphs
- ☐ Step by step
- ☐ Table or chart

WHO IS THIS FOR:

____

SPECIAL RULES:

____

____

MY NOTES:

____

____

MY AI HELPER GUIDE

PROJECT NAME:

____

DATE: ____________ TRY NUMBER: ____________

WHAT I WANT AI TO DO:

____

____

MORE DETAILS:

____

____

SHOW AN EXAMPLE:

Good example: ____________________________________

____

Bad Example: ____________________________________

____

MY STEPS: ____________________________________

____

____

MY PROMPT TO AI:

____

____

____

____

HOW IT WENT:

What was cool: ____________________________________

What needs fixing: ________________________________

Next time I will: __________________________________

MY NOTES:

____

____

MY AI HELPER GUIDE

WHAT DO I WANT HELP WITH:

____

AI SHOULD ACT LIKE:

____

PICK A HELPER:

- ☐ Friendly Teacher
- ☐ Creative Friend
- ☐ Story Helper
- ☐ Homework Buddy
- ☐ Other: _______________

HOW SHOULD IT SOUND:

- ☐ Fun and Friendly
- ☐ Excited and Encouraging
- ☐ Simple and Clear
- ☐ Super Creative
- ☐ Like a Real Expert

HOW SHOULD IT LOOK:

- ☐ List with dots
- ☐ List with numbers
- ☐ Short paragraphs
- ☐ Step by step
- ☐ Table or chart

WHO IS THIS FOR:

____

SPECIAL RULES:

____

____

MY NOTES:

____

____

MY AI HELPER GUIDE

PROJECT NAME:

____

DATE: ______________ TRY NUMBER: ______________

WHAT I WANT AI TO DO:

____

____

MORE DETAILS:

____

____

SHOW AN EXAMPLE:

Good example: ____

____

Bad Example: ____

____

MY STEPS: ____

____

____

MY PROMPT TO AI:

____

____

____

____

HOW IT WENT:

What was cool: ____

What needs fixing: ____

Next time I will: ____

MY NOTES:

____

____

MY AI HELPER GUIDE

WHAT DO I WANT HELP WITH:

____

AI SHOULD ACT LIKE:

____

PICK A HELPER:

- ☐ Friendly Teacher
- ☐ Creative Friend
- ☐ Story Helper
- ☐ Homework Buddy
- ☐ Other: _______________

HOW SHOULD IT SOUND:

- ☐ Fun and Friendly
- ☐ Excited and Encouraging
- ☐ Simple and Clear
- ☐ Super Creative
- ☐ Like a Real Expert

HOW SHOULD IT LOOK:

- ☐ List with dots
- ☐ List with numbers
- ☐ Short paragraphs
- ☐ Step by step
- ☐ Table or chart

WHO IS THIS FOR:

____

SPECIAL RULES:

____

____

MY NOTES:

____

____

MY AI HELPER GUIDE

PROJECT NAME:

____

DATE: ______________ TRY NUMBER: ______________

WHAT I WANT AI TO DO:

____

____

MORE DETAILS:

____

____

SHOW AN EXAMPLE:

Good example: ________________________________

____

Bad Example: _________________________________

____

MY STEPS: ________________________________

____

____

MY PROMPT TO AI:

____

____

____

____

HOW IT WENT:

What was cool: _______________________________

What needs fixing: ___________________________

Next time I will: _____________________________

MY NOTES:

____

____

MY AI HELPER GUIDE

WHAT DO I WANT HELP WITH:

____

AI SHOULD ACT LIKE:

____

PICK A HELPER:

- ☐ Friendly Teacher
- ☐ Creative Friend
- ☐ Story Helper
- ☐ Homework Buddy
- ☐ Other: ______________

HOW SHOULD IT SOUND:

- ☐ Fun and Friendly
- ☐ Excited and Encouraging
- ☐ Simple and Clear
- ☐ Super Creative
- ☐ Like a Real Expert

HOW SHOULD IT LOOK:

- ☐ List with dots
- ☐ List with numbers
- ☐ Short paragraphs
- ☐ Step by step
- ☐ Table or chart

WHO IS THIS FOR:

____

SPECIAL RULES:

____

____

MY NOTES:

____

____

MY AI HELPER GUIDE

PROJECT NAME:

____

DATE: ____________ TRY NUMBER: ____________

WHAT I WANT AI TO DO:

____

____

MORE DETAILS:

____

____

SHOW AN EXAMPLE:

Good example: ______________________________

____

Bad Example: _______________________________

____

MY STEPS: ______________________________

____

____

MY PROMPT TO AI:

____

____

____

____

HOW IT WENT:

What was cool: ______________________________

What needs fixing: ___________________________

Next time I will: ____________________________

MY NOTES:

____

____

MY AI HELPER GUIDE

WHAT DO I WANT HELP WITH:

____

AI SHOULD ACT LIKE:

____

PICK A HELPER:

☐ Friendly Teacher
☐ Creative Friend
☐ Story Helper
☐ Homework Buddy
☐ Other: ______________

HOW SHOULD IT SOUND:

☐ Fun and Friendly
☐ Excited and Encouraging
☐ Simple and Clear
☐ Super Creative
☐ Like a Real Expert

HOW SHOULD IT LOOK:

☐ List with dots
☐ List with numbers
☐ Short paragraphs
☐ Step by step
☐ Table or chart

WHO IS THIS FOR:

____

SPECIAL RULES:

____

____

MY NOTES:

____

____

MY AI HELPER GUIDE

PROJECT NAME:

____

DATE: ____________ TRY NUMBER: ____________

WHAT I WANT AI TO DO:

____

____

MORE DETAILS:

____

____

SHOW AN EXAMPLE:

Good example: ______________________________

____

Bad Example: _______________________________

____

MY STEPS: _______________________________

____

____

MY PROMPT TO AI:

____

____

____

____

HOW IT WENT:

What was cool: ______________________________

What needs fixing: ___________________________

Next time I will: _____________________________

MY NOTES:

____

____

MY AI HELPER GUIDE

WHAT DO I WANT HELP WITH:

____

AI SHOULD ACT LIKE:

____

PICK A HELPER:

☐ Friendly Teacher
☐ Creative Friend
☐ Story Helper
☐ Homework Buddy
☐ Other: ______________

HOW SHOULD IT SOUND:

☐ Fun and Friendly
☐ Excited and Encouraging
☐ Simple and Clear
☐ Super Creative
☐ Like a Real Expert

HOW SHOULD IT LOOK:

☐ List with dots
☐ List with numbers
☐ Short paragraphs
☐ Step by step
☐ Table or chart

WHO IS THIS FOR:

____

SPECIAL RULES:

____

____

MY NOTES:

____

____

MY AI HELPER GUIDE

PROJECT NAME:

____

DATE: ____________ TRY NUMBER: ____________

WHAT I WANT AI TO DO:

____

____

MORE DETAILS:

____

____

SHOW AN EXAMPLE:

Good example: ________________________________

____

Bad Example: _________________________________

____

MY STEPS: ________________________________

____

____

MY PROMPT TO AI:

____

____

____

____

HOW IT WENT:

What was cool: _______________________________

What needs fixing: ___________________________

Next time I will: ____________________________

MY NOTES:

____

____

MY AI HELPER GUIDE

WHAT DO I WANT HELP WITH:

____

AI SHOULD ACT LIKE:

____

PICK A HELPER:

- ☐ Friendly Teacher
- ☐ Creative Friend
- ☐ Story Helper
- ☐ Homework Buddy
- ☐ Other: ______________

HOW SHOULD IT SOUND:

- ☐ Fun and Friendly
- ☐ Excited and Encouraging
- ☐ Simple and Clear
- ☐ Super Creative
- ☐ Like a Real Expert

HOW SHOULD IT LOOK:

- ☐ List with dots
- ☐ List with numbers
- ☐ Short paragraphs
- ☐ Step by step
- ☐ Table or chart

WHO IS THIS FOR:

____

SPECIAL RULES:

____

____

MY NOTES:

____

____

MY AI HELPER GUIDE

PROJECT NAME:

____

DATE: ____________ TRY NUMBER: ____________

WHAT I WANT AI TO DO:

____

____

MORE DETAILS:

____

____

SHOW AN EXAMPLE:

Good example: ______________________________

____

Bad Example: _______________________________

____

MY STEPS: _________________________________

____

____

MY PROMPT TO AI:

____

____

____

____

HOW IT WENT:

What was cool: _____________________________

What needs fixing: __________________________

Next time I will: ____________________________

MY NOTES:

____

____

MY AI HELPER GUIDE

WHAT DO I WANT HELP WITH:

____

AI SHOULD ACT LIKE:

____

PICK A HELPER:

☐ Friendly Teacher
☐ Creative Friend
☐ Story Helper
☐ Homework Buddy
☐ Other: ______________

HOW SHOULD IT SOUND:

☐ Fun and Friendly
☐ Excited and Encouraging
☐ Simple and Clear
☐ Super Creative
☐ Like a Real Expert

HOW SHOULD IT LOOK:

☐ List with dots
☐ List with numbers
☐ Short paragraphs
☐ Step by step
☐ Table or chart

WHO IS THIS FOR:

____

SPECIAL RULES:

____

____

MY NOTES:

____

____

MY AI HELPER GUIDE

PROJECT NAME:

____

DATE: ______________ TRY NUMBER: ______________

WHAT I WANT AI TO DO:

____

____

MORE DETAILS:

____

____

SHOW AN EXAMPLE:

Good example: ____

____

Bad Example: ____

____

MY STEPS: ____

____

____

MY PROMPT TO AI:

____

____

____

____

HOW IT WENT:

What was cool: ____

What needs fixing: ____

Next time I will: ____

MY NOTES:

____

____

MY AI HELPER GUIDE

WHAT DO I WANT HELP WITH:

____

AI SHOULD ACT LIKE:

____

PICK A HELPER:

- ☐ Friendly Teacher
- ☐ Creative Friend
- ☐ Story Helper
- ☐ Homework Buddy
- ☐ Other: ____________

HOW SHOULD IT SOUND:

- ☐ Fun and Friendly
- ☐ Excited and Encouraging
- ☐ Simple and Clear
- ☐ Super Creative
- ☐ Like a Real Expert

HOW SHOULD IT LOOK:

- ☐ List with dots
- ☐ List with numbers
- ☐ Short paragraphs
- ☐ Step by step
- ☐ Table or chart

WHO IS THIS FOR:

____

SPECIAL RULES:

____

____

MY NOTES:

____

____

MY AI HELPER GUIDE

PROJECT NAME:

____

DATE: ______________ TRY NUMBER: ______________

WHAT I WANT AI TO DO:

____

____

MORE DETAILS:

____

____

SHOW AN EXAMPLE:

Good example: ______________________________

____

Bad Example: _______________________________

____

MY STEPS: ______________________________

____

____

MY PROMPT TO AI:

____

____

____

____

HOW IT WENT:

What was cool: ______________________________

What needs fixing: ___________________________

Next time I will: _____________________________

MY NOTES:

____

____

MY AI HELPER GUIDE

WHAT DO I WANT HELP WITH:

____

AI SHOULD ACT LIKE:

____

PICK A HELPER:

☐ Friendly Teacher
☐ Creative Friend
☐ Story Helper
☐ Homework Buddy
☐ Other: ____________

HOW SHOULD IT SOUND:

☐ Fun and Friendly
☐ Excited and Encouraging
☐ Simple and Clear
☐ Super Creative
☐ Like a Real Expert

HOW SHOULD IT LOOK:

☐ List with dots
☐ List with numbers
☐ Short paragraphs
☐ Step by step
☐ Table or chart

WHO IS THIS FOR:

____

SPECIAL RULES:

____

____

MY NOTES:

____

____

MY AI HELPER GUIDE

PROJECT NAME:

DATE: ______________ TRY NUMBER: ______________

WHAT I WANT AI TO DO:

MORE DETAILS:

SHOW AN EXAMPLE:

Good example:

Bad Example:

MY STEPS:

MY PROMPT TO AI:

HOW IT WENT:

What was cool:

What needs fixing:

Next time I will:

MY NOTES:

MY AI HELPER GUIDE

WHAT DO I WANT HELP WITH:

____

AI SHOULD ACT LIKE:

____

PICK A HELPER:

- ☐ Friendly Teacher
- ☐ Creative Friend
- ☐ Story Helper
- ☐ Homework Buddy
- ☐ Other: ______________

HOW SHOULD IT SOUND:

- ☐ Fun and Friendly
- ☐ Excited and Encouraging
- ☐ Simple and Clear
- ☐ Super Creative
- ☐ Like a Real Expert

HOW SHOULD IT LOOK:

- ☐ List with dots
- ☐ List with numbers
- ☐ Short paragraphs
- ☐ Step by step
- ☐ Table or chart

WHO IS THIS FOR:

____

SPECIAL RULES:

____

____

MY NOTES:

____

____

MY AI HELPER GUIDE

PROJECT NAME:

____

DATE: ____________ TRY NUMBER: ____________

WHAT I WANT AI TO DO:

____

____

MORE DETAILS:

____

____

SHOW AN EXAMPLE:

Good example: ________________________________

____

Bad Example: _________________________________

____

MY STEPS: ________________________________

____

____

MY PROMPT TO AI:

____

____

____

____

HOW IT WENT:

What was cool:________________________________

What needs fixing: ____________________________

Next time I will:______________________________

MY NOTES:

____

____

MY AI HELPER GUIDE

WHAT DO I WANT HELP WITH:

____

AI SHOULD ACT LIKE:

____

PICK A HELPER:

- ☐ Friendly Teacher
- ☐ Creative Friend
- ☐ Story Helper
- ☐ Homework Buddy
- ☐ Other: ________________

HOW SHOULD IT SOUND:

- ☐ Fun and Friendly
- ☐ Excited and Encouraging
- ☐ Simple and Clear
- ☐ Super Creative
- ☐ Like a Real Expert

HOW SHOULD IT LOOK:

- ☐ List with dots
- ☐ List with numbers
- ☐ Short paragraphs
- ☐ Step by step
- ☐ Table or chart

WHO IS THIS FOR:

____

SPECIAL RULES:

____

____

MY NOTES:

____

____

MY AI HELPER GUIDE

PROJECT NAME:

____

DATE: _____________ TRY NUMBER: _____________

WHAT I WANT AI TO DO:

____

____

MORE DETAILS:

____

____

SHOW AN EXAMPLE:

Good example: ____

____

Bad Example: ____

____

MY STEPS: ____

____

____

MY PROMPT TO AI:

____

____

____

____

HOW IT WENT:

What was cool: ____

What needs fixing: ____

Next time I will: ____

MY NOTES:

____

____

MY AI HELPER GUIDE

WHAT DO I WANT HELP WITH:

____

AI SHOULD ACT LIKE:

____

PICK A HELPER:

☐ Friendly Teacher
☐ Creative Friend
☐ Story Helper
☐ Homework Buddy
☐ Other: _______________

HOW SHOULD IT SOUND:

☐ Fun and Friendly
☐ Excited and Encouraging
☐ Simple and Clear
☐ Super Creative
☐ Like a Real Expert

HOW SHOULD IT LOOK:

☐ List with dots
☐ List with numbers
☐ Short paragraphs
☐ Step by step
☐ Table or chart

WHO IS THIS FOR:

____

SPECIAL RULES:

____

____

MY NOTES:

____

____

MY AI HELPER GUIDE

PROJECT NAME:

____

DATE: ______________ TRY NUMBER: ______________

WHAT I WANT AI TO DO:

____

____

MORE DETAILS:

____

____

SHOW AN EXAMPLE:

Good example: ______________________________________

____

Bad Example: ______________________________________

____

MY STEPS: ______________________________________

____

____

MY PROMPT TO AI:

____

____

____

____

HOW IT WENT:

What was cool: ______________________________________

What needs fixing: __________________________________

Next time I will: ___________________________________

MY NOTES:

____

____

MY AI HELPER GUIDE

WHAT DO I WANT HELP WITH:

____

AI SHOULD ACT LIKE:

____

PICK A HELPER:

☐ Friendly Teacher
☐ Creative Friend
☐ Story Helper
☐ Homework Buddy
☐ Other: ____________

HOW SHOULD IT SOUND:

☐ Fun and Friendly
☐ Excited and Encouraging
☐ Simple and Clear
☐ Super Creative
☐ Like a Real Expert

HOW SHOULD IT LOOK:

☐ List with dots
☐ List with numbers
☐ Short paragraphs
☐ Step by step
☐ Table or chart

WHO IS THIS FOR:

____

SPECIAL RULES:

____

____

MY NOTES:

____

____

MY AI HELPER GUIDE

PROJECT NAME:

____

DATE: ____________ TRY NUMBER: ____________

WHAT I WANT AI TO DO:

____

____

MORE DETAILS:

____

____

SHOW AN EXAMPLE:

Good example: ________________________________

____

Bad Example: _________________________________

____

MY STEPS: _________________________________

____

____

MY PROMPT TO AI:

____

____

____

____

HOW IT WENT:

What was cool: _______________________________

What needs fixing: ____________________________

Next time I will: _____________________________

MY NOTES:

____

____

MY AI HELPER GUIDE

WHAT DO I WANT HELP WITH:

____

AI SHOULD ACT LIKE:

____

PICK A HELPER:

- ☐ Friendly Teacher
- ☐ Creative Friend
- ☐ Story Helper
- ☐ Homework Buddy
- ☐ Other: ______________

HOW SHOULD IT SOUND:

- ☐ Fun and Friendly
- ☐ Excited and Encouraging
- ☐ Simple and Clear
- ☐ Super Creative
- ☐ Like a Real Expert

HOW SHOULD IT LOOK:

- ☐ List with dots
- ☐ List with numbers
- ☐ Short paragraphs
- ☐ Step by step
- ☐ Table or chart

WHO IS THIS FOR:

____

SPECIAL RULES:

____

____

MY NOTES:

____

MY AI HELPER GUIDE

PROJECT NAME:

____

DATE: ______________ TRY NUMBER: ______________

WHAT I WANT AI TO DO:

____

____

MORE DETAILS:

____

____

SHOW AN EXAMPLE:

Good example: ____

____

Bad Example: ____

____

MY STEPS: ____

____

____

MY PROMPT TO AI:

____

____

____

____

HOW IT WENT:

What was cool: ____

What needs fixing: ____

Next time I will: ____

MY NOTES:

____

____

MY AI HELPER GUIDE

WHAT DO I WANT HELP WITH:

____

AI SHOULD ACT LIKE:

____

PICK A HELPER:

- ☐ Friendly Teacher
- ☐ Creative Friend
- ☐ Story Helper
- ☐ Homework Buddy
- ☐ Other: ______________

HOW SHOULD IT SOUND:

- ☐ Fun and Friendly
- ☐ Excited and Encouraging
- ☐ Simple and Clear
- ☐ Super Creative
- ☐ Like a Real Expert

HOW SHOULD IT LOOK:

- ☐ List with dots
- ☐ List with numbers
- ☐ Short paragraphs
- ☐ Step by step
- ☐ Table or chart

WHO IS THIS FOR:

____

SPECIAL RULES:

____

____

MY NOTES:

____

____

MY AI HELPER GUIDE

PROJECT NAME:

____

DATE: ____________ TRY NUMBER: ____________

WHAT I WANT AI TO DO:

____

____

MORE DETAILS:

____

____

SHOW AN EXAMPLE:

Good example: ______________________________

____

Bad Example: ______________________________

____

MY STEPS: ______________________________

____

____

MY PROMPT TO AI:

____

____

____

____

HOW IT WENT:

What was cool: ______________________________

What needs fixing: ______________________________

Next time I will: ______________________________

MY NOTES:

____

____

MY AI HELPER GUIDE

WHAT DO I WANT HELP WITH:

____

AI SHOULD ACT LIKE:

____

PICK A HELPER:

- ☐ Friendly Teacher
- ☐ Creative Friend
- ☐ Story Helper
- ☐ Homework Buddy
- ☐ Other: ____________

HOW SHOULD IT SOUND:

- ☐ Fun and Friendly
- ☐ Excited and Encouraging
- ☐ Simple and Clear
- ☐ Super Creative
- ☐ Like a Real Expert

HOW SHOULD IT LOOK:

- ☐ List with dots
- ☐ List with numbers
- ☐ Short paragraphs
- ☐ Step by step
- ☐ Table or chart

WHO IS THIS FOR:

____

SPECIAL RULES:

____

____

MY NOTES:

____

____

MY AI HELPER GUIDE

PROJECT NAME:

____

DATE: ______________ TRY NUMBER: ______________

WHAT I WANT AI TO DO:

____

____

MORE DETAILS:

____

____

SHOW AN EXAMPLE:

Good example: ____

____

Bad Example: ____

____

MY STEPS: ____

____

____

MY PROMPT TO AI:

____

____

____

____

HOW IT WENT:

What was cool:____

What needs fixing: ____

Next time I will:____

MY NOTES:

____

____

MY AI HELPER GUIDE

WHAT DO I WANT HELP WITH:

____

AI SHOULD ACT LIKE:

____

PICK A HELPER:

- ☐ Friendly Teacher
- ☐ Creative Friend
- ☐ Story Helper
- ☐ Homework Buddy
- ☐ Other: ______________

HOW SHOULD IT SOUND:

- ☐ Fun and Friendly
- ☐ Excited and Encouraging
- ☐ Simple and Clear
- ☐ Super Creative
- ☐ Like a Real Expert

HOW SHOULD IT LOOK:

- ☐ List with dots
- ☐ List with numbers
- ☐ Short paragraphs
- ☐ Step by step
- ☐ Table or chart

WHO IS THIS FOR:

____

SPECIAL RULES:

____

____

MY NOTES:

____

____

MY AI HELPER GUIDE

PROJECT NAME:

____

DATE: ____________ TRY NUMBER: ____________

WHAT I WANT AI TO DO:

____

____

MORE DETAILS:

____

____

SHOW AN EXAMPLE:

Good example: ________________________________

____

Bad Example: _________________________________

____

MY STEPS: ________________________________

____

____

MY PROMPT TO AI:

____

____

____

____

HOW IT WENT:

What was cool: _______________________________

What needs fixing: ___________________________

Next time I will: ____________________________

MY NOTES:

____

____

MY AI HELPER GUIDE

WHAT DO I WANT HELP WITH:

____

AI SHOULD ACT LIKE:

____

PICK A HELPER:

☐ Friendly Teacher
☐ Creative Friend
☐ Story Helper
☐ Homework Buddy
☐ Other: ______________

HOW SHOULD IT SOUND:

☐ Fun and Friendly
☐ Excited and Encouraging
☐ Simple and Clear
☐ Super Creative
☐ Like a Real Expert

HOW SHOULD IT LOOK:

☐ List with dots
☐ List with numbers
☐ Short paragraphs
☐ Step by step
☐ Table or chart

WHO IS THIS FOR:

____

SPECIAL RULES:

____

____

MY NOTES:

____

____

MY AI HELPER GUIDE

PROJECT NAME:

____

DATE: ____________ TRY NUMBER: ____________

WHAT I WANT AI TO DO:

____

____

MORE DETAILS:

____

____

SHOW AN EXAMPLE:

Good example: ________________________________

____

Bad Example: _________________________________

____

MY STEPS:

____

____

____

MY PROMPT TO AI:

____

____

____

____

HOW IT WENT:

What was cool: _______________________________

What needs fixing: ___________________________

Next time I will: ____________________________

MY NOTES:

____

____

MY AI HELPER GUIDE

WHAT DO I WANT HELP WITH:

____

AI SHOULD ACT LIKE:

____

PICK A HELPER:

- ☐ Friendly Teacher
- ☐ Creative Friend
- ☐ Story Helper
- ☐ Homework Buddy
- ☐ Other: ______________

HOW SHOULD IT SOUND:

- ☐ Fun and Friendly
- ☐ Excited and Encouraging
- ☐ Simple and Clear
- ☐ Super Creative
- ☐ Like a Real Expert

HOW SHOULD IT LOOK:

- ☐ List with dots
- ☐ List with numbers
- ☐ Short paragraphs
- ☐ Step by step
- ☐ Table or chart

WHO IS THIS FOR:

____

SPECIAL RULES:

____

____

MY NOTES:

____

____

MY AI HELPER GUIDE

PROJECT NAME:

____

DATE: ______________ TRY NUMBER: ______________

WHAT I WANT AI TO DO:

____

____

MORE DETAILS:

____

____

SHOW AN EXAMPLE:

Good example: ____

____

Bad Example: ____

____

MY STEPS: ____

____

____

MY PROMPT TO AI:

____

____

____

____

HOW IT WENT:

What was cool: ____

What needs fixing: ____

Next time I will: ____

MY NOTES:

____

____

MY AI HELPER GUIDE

WHAT DO I WANT HELP WITH:

____

AI SHOULD ACT LIKE:

____

PICK A HELPER:

☐ Friendly Teacher
☐ Creative Friend
☐ Story Helper
☐ Homework Buddy
☐ Other: ________________

HOW SHOULD IT SOUND:

☐ Fun and Friendly
☐ Excited and Encouraging
☐ Simple and Clear
☐ Super Creative
☐ Like a Real Expert

HOW SHOULD IT LOOK:

☐ List with dots
☐ List with numbers
☐ Short paragraphs
☐ Step by step
☐ Table or chart

WHO IS THIS FOR:

____

SPECIAL RULES:

____

____

MY NOTES:

____

____

MY AI HELPER GUIDE

PROJECT NAME:

____

DATE: ______________ TRY NUMBER: ______________

WHAT I WANT AI TO DO:

____

____

MORE DETAILS:

____

____

SHOW AN EXAMPLE:

Good example: ____

____

Bad Example: ____

____

MY STEPS: ____

____

____

MY PROMPT TO AI:

____

____

____

____

HOW IT WENT:

What was cool:____

What needs fixing: ____

Next time I will:____

MY NOTES:

____

____

MY AI HELPER GUIDE

WHAT DO I WANT HELP WITH:

____

AI SHOULD ACT LIKE:

____

PICK A HELPER:

☐ Friendly Teacher
☐ Creative Friend
☐ Story Helper
☐ Homework Buddy
☐ Other: ______________

HOW SHOULD IT SOUND:

☐ Fun and Friendly
☐ Excited and Encouraging
☐ Simple and Clear
☐ Super Creative
☐ Like a Real Expert

HOW SHOULD IT LOOK:

☐ List with dots
☐ List with numbers
☐ Short paragraphs
☐ Step by step
☐ Table or chart

WHO IS THIS FOR:

____

SPECIAL RULES:

____

____

MY NOTES:

____

____

MY AI HELPER GUIDE

PROJECT NAME:

____

DATE: ______________ TRY NUMBER: ______________

WHAT I WANT AI TO DO:

____

____

MORE DETAILS:

____

____

SHOW AN EXAMPLE:

Good example: ____

____

Bad Example: ____

____

MY STEPS: ____

____

____

MY PROMPT TO AI:

____

____

____

____

HOW IT WENT:

What was cool: ____

What needs fixing: ____

Next time I will: ____

MY NOTES:

____

____

Your Bonus Digital Journal Awaits

As a thank-you for choosing this paperback journal, you're invited to enjoy a complimentary digital version designed to help you write, reflect, and plan wherever you are.

- Use it on your tablet, computer, or preferred note-taking app.
- Keep journaling while traveling, commuting, or relaxing at home.
- Revisit prompts and pages anytime for extra inspiration.

How to claim your bonus:

1. Type the link below into your browser.
2. Download your bonus Digital Journal.
3. Save a Master to your device.
4. Start journaling anytime and create multiple journals as needed.

https://dawnoneal.com/download-journal-for-tweens/

Thank you for being part of this journaling journey. May these pages bring you clarity, creativity, and moments of peace.

Made in the USA
Monee, IL
04 November 2026

67381923R00069